RESOLUTIONS TO LIFE'S ISSUES

VOLUME 1

RESOLUTIONS TO LIFE'S ISSUES

VOLUME 1

RONALD B. ENGRAM

COPYRIGHT © 2020 BY RONALD B. ENGRAM

All rights reserved. No part of this publication may be reproduced or transmitted in any form or by any means, electronic or mechanical, including photocopy, recording, or any information storage and retrieval system now known or to be invented, without written permission from the publisher, except in the case of brief quotations in critical articles and reviews. All Scriptures quoted from the Authorized King James Version unless otherwise noted.

ORDERING INFORMATION

Quantity sales. Special discounts are available on quantity purchases by corporations, associations, and others. Orders by trade bookstores and wholesalers. Please contact Ronald B. Engram at
requestprayerdaily@gmail.com

FORMATTING

Lita P. Ward, the Editorial Midwife
LPW Editing & Consulting Services, LLC
www.litapward.com

Published in the United States of America

ISBN: 978-0-9899569-2-5

DEDICATION

I dedicate this book to some very special people who inspired, encouraged, and motivated me to write this book. I pray that God uses *Resolutions To Life's Issues* to help resolve issues that many people are faced with today:

- To the Holy Spirit, my inspiration
- To my wife Emy, my motivator
- To my mother Amy Engram, my encourager
- To my sister Dr. Brenda E. Salter, my editor
- To my sister Evangelist Cynthia Cooper, my influencer
- To the late Bishop Cephas J. Hicks, my mentor
- And to my son Carlos, daughters Haidy and Elizabeth, grandchildren, and a host of other family and friends

TABLE OF CONTENTS

Dedication v
Resolution 1: Shout In The Midst Of Battle 1
Resolution 2: This Means War 4
Resolution 3: Grow As You Go 7
Resolution 4: The Power of Intercession 10
Resolution 5: The Power Of Fasting 13
Resolution 6: Where Is Your Faith? 15
Resolution 7: Commitment Of Motherhood 17
Resolution 8: Valley Vacationers 19
Resolution 9: From Subjugation To Liberation 22
Resolution 10: Character Building 24
Resolution 11: Pit Stop For Pitfalls 26
Resolution 12: When Trouble Meets Prayer 28
Resolution 13: No Cross, No Crown 30
Resolution 14: Godly Connections 33
Resolution 15: Victorious Thoughts 35
Resolution 16: What A Friend We Have In Jesus 37
Resolution 17: Distractions 39
Resolution 18: Joy In The Midst Of Suffering 42
Resolution 19: Father Knows Best 45
Resolution 20: Deal Or No Deal 48
Resolution 21: Spiritual Warfare 50
Resolution 22: Lord, Help Me To Value My Oil 53
Resolution 23: Finish Well 55
Resolution 24: Victory Through Prayer And Fasting 58
Resolution 25: Let It Be Seen 61

Resolution 26: O Give Thanks 63
Resolution 27: Down But Not Out 65
Resolution 28: Use Words Wisely 68
Resolution 29: The Joy Of The Lord Is My Strength...................... 71
Resolution 30: The Peace Of God In Midst Of Tribulations 73
Resolution 31: Facing The Giants 75
Resolution 32: Rejoice In The Lord 77
Resolution 33: A Continuous Prayer Life 79
Resolution 34: Keep Your Prayer Wheel Turning 81
Resolution 35: Take It To The Lord In Prayer 83
Resolution 36: Expect An Expected End 85
Resolution 37: Forward Looking Faith 87
Resolution 38: More Than Conquerors 90
Resolution 39: Get Back Up Again 92
Resolution 40: Stay Calm In The Storm 94
Resolution 41: Go For It Now 96
Resolution 42: All Things Are Working For Your Good................ 98
Resolution 43: Live Life Purposefully 100
Resolution 44: Win Souls For God's Kingdom 102
Resolution 45: One Step At A Time.. 104
Resolution 46: The Best Knocker.. 106
Resolution 47: Be Content.. 108
Resolution 48: Conquer What's Conquering You 110
Resolution 49: Don't Journey Without God 112
Resolution 50: My Daily Declaration.. 114
Resolution 51: New Life In Christ 116
Resolution 52: Trust The Process.. 119
Meet The Author 122

RESOLUTION 1
Shout In The Midst Of Battle

SATURATED WORD: Romans 8:28 - *And we know that all things work together for good to them that love God, to them who are the called according to his purpose.*

ISSUE: There are times in our lives when we are facing adversities and nothing is changing for the better. That's the time we must speak faith to our situations or make declarations by calling things that be not as though they were. To increase your faith, you must starve your doubts, lift your spirit, and hold on when we feel like turning loose. Some people look at your situation and what you're going through and automatically count you out, but don't fret because when they count you out, God is counting you in. How would you ever experience joy in the morning if there were no weeping to endure for a night? How could you experience sunshine if there were no midnights? Never, ever give up on God because He knows what's best for you. It might not seem like you're in the right place at the right time, but there's a purpose in your process. God delivers a special design upon your life. Maybe there's something He wants to do in you. There could be people He wants to take out of your life or some He wants to add to your life. Just because you can't see the good that's coming out of a bad situation doesn't mean that the good is not there. You must trust the word of God that all things work together for good to them that love the Lord and who are the called according to his purpose. So be productive and don't get stuck in a rut. You've got to tell yourself that you are only in a temporary state of affairs and that you are coming out of this. It takes faith when your life is turned upside down, but God specializes in things that seem impossible and when the time is right, He'll turn your life right side up.

CHALLENGE: You might be in a strange place, land, or time and have made up in your mind that when you come out of this warfare, you're going to give God praise for bringing you out. But don't wait until the battle is over, SHOUT NOW!

PERSONAL REFLECTIONS

_____
_____
_____
_____
_____

APPLICATION

_____
_____
_____
_____
_____

PERSONAL PRAYER

_____
_____
_____
_____
_____

ADDITIONAL NOTES

_____
_____
_____
_____

RESOLUTION 2

This Means War

SATURATED WORD: Ephesians 6:12 - *For we wrestle not against flesh and blood, but against principalities, against powers, against the rulers of the darkness of this world, against spiritual wickedness in high places.*

ISSUE: War is a military word which deals with a state of armed conflict between different nations or groups. It's also defined as an inward struggle, conflict, warfare, combat or battle. There is physical warfare and spiritual warfare. The physical warfare is between flesh and blood but spiritual warfare is between two kingdoms: the kingdom of satan against the kingdom of God, or the kingdom of darkness against the kingdom of light. Ephesians 6:22 says, "For we wrestle not against flesh and blood, but against principalities, against powers, against the rulers of the darkness of this world, against spiritual wickedness in high places." Spiritual warfare is the Christian concept of assuming a stand against evil forces. It is based on the belief in evil spirits which are able to intervene in human affairs. Then as Christians we repel such forces. The weapons employed in our physical military are guns, missiles, tanks and bombs. The spiritual weaponries that are utilized in the kingdom of God defensively are our loins girded about with truth, having on the breastplate of righteousness; and our feet shod with the preparation of the gospel of peace; above all, taking the shield of faith, wherewith we shall be able to quench all the fiery darts of the wicked and taking the helmet of salvation. Our spiritual offensive weapons are the sword of the Spirit, which is the word of God, praying always with all prayer and supplication in the Spirit.

Praise, preaching, and testimonies are all offensive weapons used in the kingdom of God against the satanic kingdom. In Matthew 16:18, Jesus said to Peter, "And I say also unto thee, that thou art Peter, and upon this rock I will build my church; and the gates of hell shall not prevail against it." Your reply might be, "I already know all of this!" Well, my question to you then is why are we fighting against each other when our fight is not against flesh and blood? As believers, we are all enlisted in the same army, under the same God, under the same authority, and under the same name. Our enemy, Satan, watches us take each other out, killing each other through lies, slander, verbal abuse, gossip, physical weapons and so much more. Matthew 28:18 tells us about our victory through salvation as well as our everyday victories, which adds up to victorious living in Christ. Every day victory is achieved by knowing, believing, and understanding the battles that we are enduring daily. Do you want all that God has for you on this earth right now, or do you desire to wait until you get to heaven to receive the victory and blessings?

CHALLENGE: There is a war going on between Satan and his fallen angels against Christ and His church. It is an invisible war that we fight against unseen forces. It is therefore a war which must be waged by faith and not by sight. It is a war that we cannot fight in our own strength, but only in the strength which God Himself supplies. The war is not being waged to see which side will win; God has already won the war by the death of His Son on the cross of Calvary. It is a part of God's eternal plan and purpose for his creation to bring glory and edification. The war is for our good and for God's glory.

PERSONAL REFLECTIONS

_____
_____
_____
_____
_____

APPLICATION

_____
_____
_____
_____
_____

PERSONAL PRAYER

_____
_____
_____
_____
_____

ADDITIONAL NOTES

_____
_____
_____
_____

RESOLUTION 3

Grow As You Go

SATURATED WORD: Ephesians 4:15 - *But speaking the truth in love, we should grow up in all things into Him who is the head, Christ.*

ISSUE: Many Christians do not progress or grow beyond their spiritual birth. They are justified but not sanctified. They are baptized by water, but not by the Holy Ghost. If God's intention was for us to stop growing after our spiritual birth, then He would take us on to heaven right after we get saved. His intent, however, was for us to get saved, keep growing, and become a mature Christian as we continue walking in the spirit of God. Paul said that we must travail in the spirit until Christ be truly formed in the believer. Have you had the desire for the things of God to be renewed lately? We must search ourselves and ask some hard questions: Is my relationship with God the same as it was when I first got saved? Am I still at the same place of my infancy? Do I know the Lord any better than I did when I first got saved? Do I have a closer walk with Him? Is my understanding of His word greater? These are questions we must ask ourselves with the intention of moving closer and going higher in Him. Don't allow yourself to become satisfied with where you are. Get out of the shallow and launch out into the deep. There's higher heights and deeper depths. You wouldn't be satisfied with starting out on your job and twenty years later, you're in the same place, in the same position, and receiving the same salary would you? Would you want your child to start out in the first grade and twelve years later, he's still in the first grade? Well, it's the same in your spiritual life or walk with God. We must continue to grow as we advance the kingdom of God. Continue to be sanctified, set apart, and made holy by the Spirit of God.

CHALLENGE: If you go deeper in God, you will grow deeper in Him. Dare to go beyond where you've been before. Seek God for fresh revelation. Accept new assignments for His glory. Don't get comfortable with where you are but be willing to grow as you go. Be intentional. Exercise and execute what you have learned in Him. Keep fighting the good fight of faith until God calls you home

PERSONAL REFLECTIONS

_____
_____
_____
_____
_____

APPLICATION

_____
_____
_____
_____
_____

PERSONAL PRAYER

_____
_____
_____
_____
_____

ADDITIONAL NOTES

_____
_____
_____
_____

RESOLUTION 4

The Power Of Intercession

SATURATED WORD: Zechariah 4:6 - *Then he answered and spake unto me, saying, This is the word of the LORD unto Zerubbabel, saying, 'Not by might, nor by power, but by my spirit, saith the LORD of hosts'*

ISSUE: It's time to rise up! Lift up your voice and cry out like never before! While we are sleeping, the enemy has crept in and developed strongholds over us. While we should be fighting principalities, powers, spiritual wickedness in high places, and rulers of the darkness of this world, we are fighting against each other. We are no longer watching as we pray, and the enemy has trespassed into our homes, jobs, relationships, bodies, minds, finances and much more. We spend more time complaining to each other about issues rather than telling God about them through prayer and intercession. Each believer has a "before" and "after"... before and after we got saved. Many of us were messed up from the floor up, but somebody was praying and interceding on our behalf for our salvation and deliverance. Therefore, we must not have the spirit of Jonah, but should want to see all come to the Lord and be delivered from the power of darkness. God has given us power and authority against the enemy in Jesus name. We must call upon the power of God and use the name of Jesus against Satanic attacks. We must frustrate Satan by using our authority against him. Satan can't prevail or stand against our authority when we exercise our faith in Jesus Christ. We must pray that the power of God be manifested each time we pray. We as intercessors must travail in the spirit as we intercede and believe that whatever weapons formed against us cannot, shall not, stand or prosper. They shall become null and void.

CHALLENGE: Calling all intercessors! Our churches, children, schools, economic systems, sick bodies and minds need us. We already have the answer! It's called prayer and intercession! We must get back to it as they are depending on us!

PERSONAL REFLECTIONS

_____
_____
_____
_____
_____

APPLICATION

_____
_____
_____
_____
_____

PERSONAL PRAYER

_____
_____
_____
_____
_____

ADDITIONAL NOTES

_____
_____
_____
_____

RESOLUTION 5

The Power Of Fasting

SATURATED WORD: Daniel 10:3 - *I ate no pleasant food, neither came meat nor wine in my mouth, neither did I anoint myself at all, till the three whole weeks were fulfilled.*

ISSUE: What caused Daniel to receive his answer to prayer? What broke the force of the delayer? Have you been waiting on an answer that's been delayed? Do you desire to know God's will for your life more clearly? Do you want to know how to react to critical situations you're facing? Then let's consider carefully the answers to these questions. Daniel walked very close to God as many of you do. He had a consistent prayer life like many of you do. He was very stern in his worship like many of you do. But what about your life of FASTING? How has it been in the past month? How consistent have you been? Have you made fasting a priority and a lifestyle? Well, when Daniel was in Babylonian captivity, his fasting brought about the open reward of God's blessing to impart great wisdom to him. He was grieved with the revelation he received from God for Israel, so he fasted for three weeks. Then he described the angel that was charged to him, which had been delayed by the prince of Persia for twenty-one days with the answer Daniel sought. His FAST BROKE the power of the delayer and Daniel received his reply from God so that his purpose could be revealed and served. There was a critical situation at hand, but fasting caused God to target Daniel's request and he received his answer.

CHALLENGE: If there's something you need God to target in your life, such as your marriage, finances, children, job, or even a closer walk with him, then add fasting to your prayers and see the FAST BREAK the power of the enemy who has been holding up your blessings.

PERSONAL REFLECTIONS

_____
_____
_____
_____

_____

APPLICATION

_____
_____
_____
_____
_____

PERSONAL PRAYER

_____
_____
_____
_____
_____

ADDITIONAL NOTES

_____
_____
_____
_____

RESOLUTION 6
Where Is Your Faith?

SATURATED WORD: Hebrews 11:1 - *Now faith is the substance of things hoped for and the evidence of things not seen.*

ISSUE: Where is your faith is a question not meant to condemn or bring indictment upon you, but rather cause you to examine where it lies as it pertains to trusting God. Your faith is greatly revealed when you are tested in a trial or going through great tribulations. As long as you are rowing your boat gently down the stream and singing merrily, merrily, merrily, merrily, life is but a dream. Life is good, but can you still sing that same old song when all of a sudden the gentle stream turns into a perfect storm and the boat you're in is beaten by contrary winds? When we step out in our daily lives facing the unknown, many times we find ourselves in the most sudden and unexpected storms. We must learn to recognize Jesus in every one of them, regardless of the circumstances, knowing that he comes with power and demonstration to see us through.

CHALLENGE: Each person has a measure of faith and God wants us to use all that we have. We must learn to handle our fears and not allow our fears to handle us. Don't allow your storms to get the best of you. Walk in the assurance that the Savior will always be there to carry you through.

PERSONAL REFLECTIONS

_____
_____
_____
_____
_____

APPLICATION

_____
_____
_____
_____
_____

PERSONAL PRAYER

_____
_____
_____
_____
_____

ADDITIONAL NOTES

_____
_____
_____
_____

RESOLUTION 7

Commitment Of Motherhood

SATURATED WORD: Proverbs 22:6 - *Train up a child in the way he should go; even when he is old, he will not depart from it.*

ISSUE: Mother's Day is such a special holiday because mothers themselves are so special. There is a very special bond between a mother and her child like none other. We love our dads and we certainly turn to them for security and strength, but there's a special connection or bonding between a mother and her child. A good mother makes a difference and makes up the difference wherever there's a deficit. Mothers almost never have a carefree moment because they are constantly engaged in the welfare and deep concerns of their children's everyday life. It's been said that a mother is only as happy as her least happy child. Many trade in their happiness for the tears that their children shed. The reason why a mother hurts so when her child does wrong is because of the love she has for her child. I understand that there are numerous people who have raised children according to God's plan, did everything they knew to do to raise them right, and yet when they became older they went against their training. It's not always bad parenting that causes the child to go astray. Your task as a mother is to teach them the right way and live a Godly life before them, but God is the one who gives the increase and reveals himself to them.

CHALLENGE: A mother's responsibility is to take her children before the throne in prayer and God takes it from there. Persevere mothers; don't give up on training and praying for your children. Release yourself from guilt and bondage and trust God for their future. Remember, train up a child in the way he should go; even when he is old he will not depart from it.

PERSONAL REFLECTIONS

APPLICATION

PERSONAL PRAYER

ADDITIONAL NOTES

RESOLUTION 8
Valley Vacationers

SATURATED WORD: 1 Kings 20:28 - *Because the Syrians have said, The Lord is God of the hills, but he is not God of the valleys, therefore will I deliver all this great multitude into thine hand, and ye shall know that I am the Lord.*

ISSUE: Many of us like going up into the mountains because of its peacefulness, serenity, and tranquility. It's a good place to get away to relax your body, collect your thoughts, clear your mind and receive revelations from God. It was on the Mountain of Ararat that God made a covenant with Noah, Mt. Moriah where Solomon built his temple, Mt. Sinai where Moses received the Ten Commandments, Mt. Carmel where Elijah won in a duel against the false prophets of Baal, Mt. Zion where David built Jerusalem, and the Mt. of Olives where Jesus taught his disciples. God gives us mountain top experiences in order to sustain us as we go down into the valley! His revelation is always intended to help us journey with Him more closely on the road ahead. For Moses, that journey was to lead God's people to the Promised Land. For Elijah, it was to confront wickedness in the land. For Jesus, it was the journey to the cross to redeem man from the penalty of sin. And for us, it is a journey from a world of chaos to a promised place of eternal glory with God. In life we have to pass through an infinite diversity of circumstances and they are not always mountain top experiences. There are valleys, sometimes very deep valleys that we often encounter. Simply because you have valley experiences doesn't mean you can't have victory there, because the same God that grants you victory in the mountains is the same God who will grant you victory in the valley. Valleys are for us to pass through, not to settle there. Unfortunately, many of us go too deep and stay too long.

Some build vacation homes there staying weeks, months, even years at a time. They vacation in the valley of depression, hopelessness, despair, grief, discouragement, anxiety and mourning, but tell yourself while in the valley that the same God that granted me victory in the mountain will give me victory in the valley. It's wholly a piece of life's journey.

CHALLENGE: While you're going through your valley experiences, know that the God who, having begun a good work in you will perform it until the day of Jesus Christ. Know that the God who wants you and me to get the maximum out of those valley experiences in His wisdom is working all things out together for good, to them that love Him, who are the called according to his purpose

PERSONAL REFLECTIONS

_____
_____
_____
_____
_____

APPLICATION

_____
_____
_____
_____
_____

PERSONAL PRAYER

_____
_____
_____
_____
_____

ADDITIONAL NOTES

_____
_____
_____
_____

RESOLUTION 9

From Subjugation To Liberation

SATURATED WORD: Exodus 3:8 - *And I am come down to deliver them out of the hand of the Egyptians, and to bring them.....unto a land flowing with milk and honey.....*

ISSUE: Subjugation means to dominate or control. Liberation means being set free from imprisonment or slavery. God led Israel into Canaan, a liberating place, after being held in Egypt, a subjugating place. Canaan was a land flowing with milk and honey while Egypt was a place of captivity, slavery and bondage. The way you recognize if you're in the right place or not is by the evidence you bring from it. From Canaan, the evidence of grapes was so large until it required two men to carry a single cluster upon a pole to bring it out. From Egypt, the children of Israel brought out over 400 years of captivity, bondage and slavery. What evidence are you bringing out of what you're into? Blessing or bondage? Favor or failure? Joy or bitterness? Happiness or sadness? The Israelites were held captive by Pharaoh, but Moses under the command and authority of God was sent as His oracle. He said to Pharaoh, the God of Abraham, Isaac and Jacob said, let my people go. As a child of God you've been afforded that same authority. Tell the Pharaohs of sickness, shaky finances, and troubled marriages, to let my children go, my marriage go, my finances go, my good health go, my good name go, my mind go, my peace go, and my joy go.

CHALLENGE: What evidence is coming out of your life? Are you living a life of freedom or bondage? Let there be evidence that God has brought you from a life of subjugation to a life of liberation. Whom the Son sets free is free indeed.

PERSONAL REFLECTIONS

_____
_____
_____
_____
_____

APPLICATION

_____
_____
_____
_____
_____

PERSONAL PRAYER

_____
_____
_____
_____
_____

ADDITIONAL NOTES

_____
_____
_____
_____

RESOLUTION 10
Character Building

SATURATED WORD: Romans 5:3-4 - *More than that, we rejoice in our sufferings, knowing that suffering produces endurance, and endurance produces character, and character produces hope.*

ISSUE: Character is who you are. It defines you and guides your action, hopefully in a positive way. Character is a description of a person's attributes, traits and abilities. It impacts a person's honesty and loyalty. It defines who a person truly is. In building character, choose a set of morals and principles that you believe will lead to a satisfying and righteous life and live by them. Decide what you must do in your behavior to align your life more closely to what you believe. Be conscious every day of the decisions you make, big or small, and how close they bring you into being the person you really want to become. Appreciate your own values. Focus on the positive in life and spend very little time on the negative. Always be truthful in all things because dishonesty is an assault against your own character. Excel where you are, and do your best in whatever you practice.

CHALLENGE: Beware of people who'll attempt to convince you to give up on your character telling you that nobody's perfect. The fact that nobody's perfect doesn't mean violating what you believe to be right. It's good to learn from your mistakes, but you don't always have to make mistakes in order to learn.

PERSONAL REFLECTIONS

_____
_____
_____
_____
_____

APPLICATION

_____
_____
_____
_____
_____

PERSONAL PRAYER

_____
_____
_____
_____
_____

ADDITIONAL NOTES

_____
_____
_____
_____

RESOLUTION 11

Pit Stop For Pitfalls

SATURATED WORD: Psalm 34:19 - *Many are the afflictions of the righteous, But the LORD delivers him out of them all.*

ISSUE: Has your life been the pits lately? Have you been experiencing more downs than up? Does the wind keep on blowing in your life? Have things gotten worse rather than better? Well, don't let life get you down. You must tell yourself that it won't always be this way. Sometime you might feel like throwing in the towel and giving up but I encourage you to remain in the race; you're merely a pit stop away from your turnaround. Many things happen on the tracks of life. You can be riding along with everything going well, and all of sudden a problem rear ends you or some issue comes along and sideswipes you. Or maybe you threw a rod because you got overheated and lost your cool. Well, maybe it's time for a pit stop to get some adjustments made. There's a pit crew standing by waiting: The Father, Son, and the Holy Ghost will be there to assist you. Your pit stop might be in your prayer closet, for the effectual fervent prayers of the righteous availeth much. Maybe it's in your praise… when praises go up, blessings come down. Maybe it's in your fasting…this kind comes only by prayer and fasting. God is only a call away to come to your rescue.

CHALLENGE: If you find yourself having a pit fit or pit fall, just make a pit stop. The pit crew will be there waiting to mobilize you again.

PERSONAL REFLECTIONS

_____
_____
_____
_____
_____

APPLICATION

_____
_____
_____
_____
_____

PERSONAL PRAYER

_____
_____
_____
_____
_____

ADDITIONAL NOTES

_____
_____
_____
_____

RESOLUTION 12

When Trouble Meets Prayer

SATURATED WORD: James 5:16 *The effectual fervent prayer of a righteous man availeth much.*

ISSUE: Prayer brings you into the presence of God and God in the presence of you. You need Him when you're in trouble and even when trouble isn't troubling you. No one can claim exempt status when it comes to trouble. Trouble doesn't have to come knocking at your door because it has already made its way in. As you look around, you see trouble in marriages, relationships, finances, jobs, politics, and spirituality. There's trouble in the White House, black house, poor house, and even the church house. The answer to trouble is found in God's "how." His "how" is found in His word. His word is filled with promises and all of His promises are yes and amen. When looking for solutions to trouble, you must go to God who is the source of every resource. He has unlimited, available supply to meet your every need. He can work miracles in your life through the power of saying "let there be." He's the God of eternity who has unlimited power and infinite values that cannot be measured by time. He will do for you what you can't do for yourself. You are hopeless and helpless without Him. You need Him in every situation. In spite of trials, tribulations, or afflictions, just be encouraged because God promised to deliver you out of them all. It's not God's will that you be troubled. You can be in trouble without being troubled. Jesus' stripes healed you from being troubled. John 14:1 says, "Let not your heart be troubled: ye believe in God, believe also in me."

CHALLENGE: Making prayer your priority is the gateway towards getting your needs met. Tell God about your trouble and your trouble about God.

PERSONAL REFLECTIONS

___

APPLICATION

___

PERSONAL PRAYER

___

ADDITIONAL NOTES

___

RESOLUTION 13

No Cross, No Crown

SATURATED WORD: John 10:10 - *The thief cometh not, but for to steal, and to kill, and to destroy: I am come that they might have life, and that they might have it more abundantly.*

ISSUE: We see two opposing forces in our text, the kingdom of God and the Satanic kingdom. In the satanic kingdom, Satan has evil in mind: he is called a thief that comes to steal, kill and destroy. On the other hand, in the kingdom of God; God has good in mind. If you look in the word <u>devil</u>, you get <u>evil</u> out of it. Out of <u>good,</u> you get <u>God</u> out if it. So the devil is evil and God is good. If there is no cross, there can be no crown. When we experience painful situations, we are prompted to make sacrifices we would not normally make to achieve the greater good. Pain and sacrifice are integral parts of the Christian experience. That's why Jesus encourages every believer with an accounting term, <u>count the cost</u>. The promise of eternal life would not come without the pain of the cross. Before the crown, there must be a cross. There are many who have been knocked down in every round of life: lost jobs, broken marriages, failures, and various disappointments of life. They have been dealt some very powerful punches that have floored even the strongest believers. But as you wait on God to move on your behalf, don't spend time staring at the calendar… a watched pot never boils. Do something while you wait. Those who are busy in kingdom building activities find that it is easier to wait. Don't panic, give up, or throw in the towel; God will see you through. Just remember that while you're carrying your cross, you're working on your crown. "No cross, no crown."

CHALLENGE: Our fear sees the worst that can happen. Our faith knows the best that can happen. Our faith remembers that as long as God is with us, He will make a way for us.

PERSONAL REFLECTIONS

_____
_____
_____
_____

_____

APPLICATION

_____
_____
_____
_____
_____

PERSONAL PRAYER

_____
_____
_____
_____
_____

ADDITIONAL NOTES

_____
_____
_____
_____

RESOLUTION 14
Godly Connections

SATURATED WORD: Psalm 1:1 - *Blessed is the man who walketh not in the counsel of the ungodly, nor standeth in the way of sinners, nor sitteth in the seat of the scornful.*

ISSUE: It's alright to do networking, but don't find yourself netting with people in the wrong kind of work. People who do not make regular deposits into your life will eventually begin making regular withdrawals and will deplete you. People who do not add to your life will constantly subtract from it. Don't allow anyone to hold you back when you're trying to move forward. You can't take certain people from your past with you into your future because they will sometimes try to block, alter, or sabotage you before reaching your destiny. You have a Godly purpose to fulfill, and not everyone wants to see it come to pass. You don't know how much longer you have, because the night is quickly coming to an end when no man can work. So spend quality time fulfilling your kingdom assignments because time is winding up.

CHALLENGE: You've got to be able to recognize a Godly connection. God will send Godly people into your life only for the purpose of helping you walk into your Divine purpose and destiny. They don't want anything from you. They know that they are only there to help you achieve your kingdom assignment.

PERSONAL REFLECTIONS

_____
_____
_____
_____
_____

APPLICATION

_____
_____
_____
_____
_____

PERSONAL PRAYER

_____
_____
_____
_____
_____

ADDITIONAL NOTES

_____
_____
_____
_____

RESOLUTION 15

What A Friend We Have In Jesus

SATURATED WORD: Proverbs 18:24 - *A man that hath friends must shew himself friendly: and there is a friend that sticketh closer than a brother.*

ISSUE: Jesus had no earthly home. He could not claim homestead exemption, be a part of the neighborhood watch, or pay subdivision association fees, because this world was not His home. He was just here on assignment, driven by purpose, doing the will of the Father that sent Him. He is a friend that sticks closer than a brother. You can call Him morning, noon, or night because He never sleeps nor slumbers. You can cast all of your cares upon Him because He cares for you. He saves, heals, delivers, provides, and so much more. If you are conformed to this world, He can transform you by the renewing of your mind. If your mind is miserable, your eyes envious, your conversations corrupt, your soul sinful, your heart harden, your path perverted, your ways wretched, your desires detestable, your thoughts terrible, your wants worldly, your purpose polluted, your life lustful, your imagination impure, then let me introduce you to Jesus. He's a friend of friends. When you come in contact with Him, the drunk becomes sober, the liar becomes truthful, the proud becomes humble, the hateful becomes loving, the foolish becomes wise, the thief becomes honest, the unthankful becomes grateful, the troubled becomes peaceful, the rude becomes kind, the lost becomes saved, and the list goes on.

CHALLENGE: Your highest pursuit in life should be to get to know Jesus. The way to accomplish that is through salvation, relationship, and intimacy. He came into this world to redeem us from every penalty of sin. He's not only our King and Savior, but He's also our friend. Wow! What a friend we have in Jesus!!!

PERSONAL REFLECTIONS

_____
_____
_____
_____
_____

APPLICATION

_____
_____
_____
_____
_____

PERSONAL PRAYER

_____
_____
_____
_____
_____

ADDITIONAL NOTES

_____
_____
_____
_____

RESOLUTION 16
Victorious Thoughts

SATURATED WORD: Philippians 4:8 - *Finally, brethren, whatsoever things are true, whatsoever things are honest, whatsoever things are just, whatsoever things are pure, whatsoever things are lovely, whatsoever things are of good report; if there be any virtue, and if there be any praise, think on these things.*

ISSUE: Look for things that are good and meditate on them. This verse tells us to look for the lovely while living in a sometimes loveless world. If we do this, we will be encouraged and strengthened. You will be challenged from day to day with the thoughts you think. We are not promised that our days will always be blissful and peaceful. As you go through each day, you may encounter things which make you cringe. Deal with these things as you must, but do not let them become your focus. Remember that the almighty God is with you. Remind yourself of how faithful He has been in your life and set your gauge in that direction. God will be faithful again because it is his character. Don't allow the enemy to tell you that you can't hear God, or that God doesn't speak to you because He does speak to us. We have to tune our ears to His frequency by spending time with Him to recognize His voice.

CHALLENGE: A focused mind will bring clarity in your life. Your mind is the battleground of your enemy Satan, but your weapon for victory is the word of God as in Philippians 4:8. There might be adjustments to be made, but that small sacrifice can make the difference in the very quality of your life.

PERSONAL REFLECTIONS

_____
_____
_____
_____

_____

APPLICATION

_____
_____
_____
_____
_____

PERSONAL PRAYER

_____
_____
_____
_____
_____

ADDITIONAL NOTES

_____
_____
_____
_____

RESOLUTION 17
Distractions

SATURATED WORD: 2 Corinthians 10:5 - *Casting down imaginations, and every high thing that exalteth itself against the knowledge of God, and bringing into captivity every thought to the obedience of Christ.*

ISSUE: Negative images in your mind can produce distractions. Distraction is anything that precludes you from devoting your full attention to what should be a priority in your life. Images are what you picture or visualize mentally. What images are you carrying around in your mind? Are they images of victory or defeat? Sickness or wellness? Wealth or poverty? Romans 8:37 says, "Yet in all these things we are more than conquerors through Him who loved us." Therefore, we have the ability to conquer negative thoughts and images that come in our mind. It's just as easy and more profitable to think on things as Philippians 4:8 says: "whatsoever things are true, whatsoever things are honest, whatsoever things are just, whatsoever things are pure, whatsoever things are lovely, whatsoever things are of good report; if there be any virtue, and if there be any praise, think on these things." So we have the ability to decide what images are placed in our minds. Negative thoughts and images are all distractions that bring about doubt, unbelief, depression, oppression, compression, designed to deter us from the plan and purpose of God for our lives. 2 Corinthians 10:5 says that we should "Cast down imaginations, and every high thing that exalteth itself against the knowledge of God, and bringing into captivity every thought to the obedience of Christ." Therefore, we are to arrest our negative thoughts, not just give them a life sentence, but put them to death.

CHALLENGE: Create the right atmosphere in your mind. God needs your full attention. The only way that you can give it is with a clear mind, free of distractions. Distractions can terrorize you. They can bring failure to your life if you let them linger long enough. Finally, get rid of them so that you can excel and reach your fullest potential.

PERSONAL REFLECTIONS

_____
_____
_____
_____
_____

APPLICATION

_____
_____
_____
_____
_____

PERSONAL PRAYER

_____
_____
_____
_____
_____

ADDITIONAL NOTES

_____
_____
_____
_____

RESOLUTION 18

Joy In The Midst Of Suffering

SATURATED WORD: Psalms 30:5 -... *weeping may endure for a night but joy cometh in the morning.*

ISSUE: The difference between joy and happiness is that happiness is dependent upon what is happening while joy is dependent upon your faith and trust in Jesus. This joy is not accomplished through man's humanity but through God's Divinity. The matters that are impossible with men are possible with God. Like a skilled surgeon, God takes out one thing and replaces it with another. He takes out fear and replaces it with faith. He takes out hate and replaces it with love. He takes out weakness and replaces it with strength. He takes out sadness and replaces it with joy. Joy is when you can have a problem, but the problem doesn't have you. God doesn't simply want us to look good outwardly, but He spends much time refining and working on us inwardly. He hand-picked you and is crafting you each and every day. He's still assembling you. His desire is that you are anxious for nothing but rather that you rest in His word. Entering into His rest is the challenge presented to you today, especially while waiting on some type of resolve to your problems. Just remember that there are no expiration dates on God's promises. To experience joy in suffering, your mind must stop doubting and rehearsing the "what if" scenarios and realize that whatever the situation, when the dust settles, you can rest in God's word. Tough times produce tough people. They teach us endurance, steadfastness, and perseverance. You can't really know the depth of your character until you know how to react under pressure. Instead of doubting and complaining about your struggles, see them as opportunities for growth. God promised to be with you, to strengthen and help you to endure them.

CHALLENGE: Knowing that Christ still reigns and has everything under control, you can rejoice even in the midst of suffering. For weeping may endure for a night, but joy cometh in the morning.

PERSONAL REFLECTIONS

APPLICATION

PERSONAL PRAYER

ADDITIONAL NOTES

RESOLUTION 19

Father Knows Best

SATURATED WORD: Proverbs 3:5-6 - *Trust in the Lord with all thine heart; and lean not unto thine own understanding. In all thy ways acknowledge him and he will direct thy path.*

ISSUE: "In all thy ways acknowledge Him." Men should not depend upon their own wisdom and understanding because we are limited. We acknowledge God not only in acts of worship or in great crisis, but in all our ways. Many people turn to God and acknowledge Him by their prayers and supplications in times of great anxiety, distress, or danger; but the true servant of God continually acknowledges Him even without an emergency or crisis but as a constant way of life, never deviating from it. We trust Him by putting our confidence in Him. He's where our faith is placed while abandoning our own understanding. Since God is superior to us, we are not to partially trust Him but do it wholeheartedly. When we have important decisions to make, we sometimes have it hard finding someone we can trust, but the Father knows what's best for us. He is a better judge of what we need than we ourselves. We must trust Him completely in every choice we make. We must not be wise in our own eyes but be willing to listen to and be corrected by God's word and wise counsel.

CHALLENGE: We are to bring our decisions to God in prayer, use the Bible as our guide, and then follow His leading because the FATHER KNOWS BEST. He will direct your paths by both guiding and protecting you. The confidence we have in Him is that He is the same yesterday, today, and forevermore. He's no respecter of person. Even when you don't understand things, your faith in Him must precede your problems. Forever be confident and without doubt that even when we can't trace Him, we must trust that our "FATHER KNOWS BEST."

PERSONAL REFLECTIONS

_____
_____
_____
_____
_____

APPLICATION

_____
_____
_____
_____
_____

PERSONAL PRAYER

_____
_____
_____
_____
_____

ADDITIONAL NOTES

_____
_____
_____
_____

RESOLUTION 20

Deal Or No Deal

SATURATED WORD: Genesis 2:16-17 - ... *for in the day that thou eatest thereof, thou shalt surely die.*

ISSUE: Deals are made or turned down every day in many places. Some are straight and some are not. In every case you must determine "Deal Or No Deal". One tree in the garden of Eden was off limit to Adam and Eve called the tree of the knowledge of good and evil. Sadly, they didn't pause to think about the consequences of their action, but instead went ahead and took a bad deal. Isn't it something, how you can get caught up in a bad deal and blame everybody else but yourself? Adam said, the woman you gave me, made me to eat of the fruit from the forbidden tree. Thus, the consequences of accepting such a bad deal caused sin to enter into the world. If Adam and Eve could speak to us now, I believe they would tell us that anything that goes against the word of God comes from the devil, and regardless of how enticing it might be, you must tell the devil, "No Deal".

CHALLENGE: Jesus came from heaven to earth to become our deal breaker with the devil but was betrayed by Judas Iscariot who accepted a deal of 32 pieces of silver and was denied by Peter not once, not twice, but thrice. But what they didn't understand was that Jesus came to die for the sins of the whole world. He became the answer to our sin problem. Now everyone has an equal opportunity to turn a bad deal into a blessing. Whosoever will, let him come. By accepting Jesus as your personal savior, you can go from being a sinner to being redeemed by the Savior because of His atonement by faith through the grace of salvation. Now that you have all of the facts, you must now make a choice, "Deal Or No Deal."

PERSONAL REFLECTIONS

_____
_____
_____
_____
_____

APPLICATION

_____
_____
_____
_____
_____

PERSONAL PRAYER

_____
_____
_____
_____
_____

ADDITIONAL NOTES

_____
_____
_____
_____

RESOLUTION 21

Spiritual Warfare

SATURATED WORD: Ephesians 6:12 - *For we wrestle not against flesh and blood, but against principalities, against powers, against the rulers of the darkness of this world, against spiritual wickedness in high places.*

ISSUE: David's skills and expertise were gained as God placed him in the midst of a variety of battles ranging from encounters with bears and lions, to his confrontation with Goliath. So what we can learn from David's life experiences is that the only way that you can become a skillful warrior is to be placed in the midst of a battle. Only when you are placed in the furnace of affliction that you can truly be trained in the art of strategic prayer and spiritual warfare. Remember, it is only when you are placed in the middle of a battle or impossible situation, and there is no one or nothing that can save you but God that a true warrior is born. Instead of giving up, giving in, or falling prey to the schemes of the enemy, consider your time of struggle, testing and temptation as Divine opportunities to be trained in the art of strategic prayer and spiritual warfare. Be assured that these times of training that God has selected will bring you into true dominion. As it was for David, they just might be the very grounds that God uses to train you for the ultimate, which is the maximization of your potential and the fulfillment of your purpose.

CHALLENGE: Be encouraged that whatever you are going through, put your trust in God. Speak words of life because we know that death and life are in the power of the tongue. Tell the devil that greater is He that is in you than he that is in the world. With His stripes I am healed. God promised me that He would never leave me nor forsake me. When you're lonely and it seems that God is not there, remember that He is your present help in times of trouble.

PERSONAL REFLECTIONS

APPLICATION

PERSONAL PRAYER

ADDITIONAL NOTES

RESOLUTION 22

Lord, Help Me To Value My Oil

SATURATED WORD: 2 King 4:7 - *Then she came and told the man of God. And he said, Go, sell the oil, and pay thy debt, and live thou and thy children of the rest.*

ISSUE: This woman almost missed her blessing because she couldn't see what was right in front of her. She didn't value her oil. Things had gotten so bad until the creditors came to take her two sons for bondsmen. She said to Elisha, "The only thing I have in the house is a jar of oil." Life can so cloud your mind until you can't see the value of what you do have. My challenge to you today is not to look at what you don't have but see the blessings in what you do have. We must ask ourselves today, do I have oil in my house? Oil represents joy and the anointing. Then the next time you're tempted to become depressed or sad because of life's difficulties, pour out a little oil of joy that you're housing inside of you and watch a continuous flow and still have some left. When your well has run dry, keep on doing what God has anointed you for and see the oil continue to flow.

CHALLENGE: When you can realize you still have a little joy or anointing oil left, use what you have unto the glory of God and watch a continuous flow.

PERSONAL REFLECTIONS

APPLICATION

PERSONAL PRAYER

ADDITIONAL NOTES

RESOLUTION 23
Finish Well

SATURATED WORD: Philippians 3:12-14 - *Not as though I had already attained, either were already perfect: but I follow after, if that I may apprehend that for which also I am apprehended of Christ Jesus. Brethren, I count not myself to have apprehended: but this one thing I do, forgetting those things which are behind, and reaching forth unto those things which are before, I press toward the mark for the prize of the high calling of God in Christ Jesus.*

ISSUE: Many have won gold medals only to find out that they had taken steroids or other illegal drugs and have had to give their medals back resulting in them not finishing well. I believe that if there was really such a thing as a time machine, most of us would gladly go back into time and correct a few things, do things differently, make some changes, or delete some things.

Even though there's not a time machine where you can pull a lever and go back into time and change some things, God has made a simple way for you to go back into time and get some things right. That way is called repentance. If you repent, God will go back into time and delete things from your past and never remember them again. Remember, it's not how you start out, but it's how you end up. Maybe your life didn't start out well. It's never too late for it to end up well.

2 Chronicles 7:14 says, "If my people, which are called by my name, shall humble themselves, and pray, and seek my face, and turn from their wicked ways; then will I hear from heaven, and will forgive their sin, and will heal their land." The land is sick with a virus called sin. Sin left untreated leads to everlasting destruction. Repentance through the blood of Jesus Christ is the only solution for

sin. This is how you finish well. So get right with God and do it now. Remember, it's not how you start out, but it's how you end up.

Jeremiah 29:11 says, "For I know the thoughts that I think toward you, saith the Lord, thoughts of peace, and not of evil, to give you an expected end." Where is your expected end?

CHALLENGE: Maybe you didn't start out right, but you can FINISH WELL. Romans 10:9-10 says, "That if thou shalt confess with thy mouth the Lord Jesus, and shalt believe in thine heart that God hath raised him from the dead, thou shalt be saved. For with the heart man believeth unto righteousness; and with the mouth confession is made unto salvation. This is your time; this is your opportunity to finish well!

PERSONAL REFLECTIONS

_____
_____
_____
_____
_____

APPLICATION

_____
_____
_____
_____
_____

PERSONAL PRAYER

_____
_____
_____
_____
_____

ADDITIONAL NOTES

_____
_____
_____
_____

RESOLUTION 24

Victory Through Prayer & Fasting

SATURATED WORD: Isaiah 58:6 - *[Is] not this the fast that I have chosen? To loose the bands of wickedness, to undo the heavy burdens, and to let the oppressed go free, and that ye break every yoke?*

ISSUE: For the past few years in January, we at the Ash St. COGIC have entered into the 21 days Daniel Fast. Many great testimonies have been given as a result of it. I believe that as you make great sacrifices at the beginning of the year you're building a foundation and setting a precedence for the rest of the year. Twenty-one days of prayer and fasting really stretches you, humbles you, prepare you for spiritual warfare, brings about revival, give you a spiritual tune-up, make you more sensitive to the Holy Spirit, helps break strongholds in your life, and helps target important decisions that you must make this year. Three important things you must designate a time for during your fasting are: 1. Praying, 2. Reading your Bible, 3. Worship.

Ephesians 4:12 declares that a three-fold cord is not easily broken.

Some things that you need deliverance from will only come forth but by prayer and fasting according to Mark 9:29.

If you want to be delivered through prayer and fasting, you must:

1. Renounce any control over your life.

2. Acknowledge what's holding you bound.

3. Forgive others and yourself.

4. Submit to the authority of God.

5. Take ownership of what you've done that needs to change.

Results of prayer and fasting:

1. Bring intimacy with God.

2. Solve problems.

3. Bring revelation.

4. Bring power.

5. Help you to know the will of God for your life.

CHALLENGE: So if you're tired of being sick and tired, if you want to experience true victory in your life, if you're tired of feeling defeated, you really want to break through, break forth, and break out of living a life of bondage, then set a time this month for prayer and fasting, one that will stretch you. And in doing so, it's going to strengthen you. Make the sacrifice up front and reap the benefits and rewards as a result.

PERSONAL REFLECTIONS

APPLICATION

PERSONAL PRAYER

ADDITIONAL NOTES

RESOLUTION 25
Let It Be Seen

SATURATED WORD: 1 Corinthians 2:9 - *But as it is written, Eye hath not seen, nor ear heard, neither have entered into the heart of man, the things which God hath prepared for them that love him.*

ISSUE: Are you living a dark, dim life of discontentment because of trials, tribulations, loss, emotional issues or trauma? If so, you are a great candidate for a bright future! Eye hath not seen, nor ear heard, neither have entered into the heart of man, the things which God hath prepared for them that love him. So many wonderful things come to you when you have the love of God in your heart. Some things you've heard, but haven't seen because God is still working on your heart. Before entering into your new year, let go of all of the negative things you're holding on to. Free yourself of anything of the past and lunge forward towards the future. Make positive declarations. Follow through and live up to them.

CHALLENGE: Jeremiah 29:11 says, "For I know the thoughts that I think towards you, saith the Lord, thoughts of peace, and not of evil, to give you an expected end." You really do have a bright future, but it's all up to you to follow through! What's standing in your way? What's holding you back? Don't think that you have to accomplish these things on your own. Jesus is your present help and is standing by waiting to hear from you. Now is a good time to give him a call. Let your dreams be seen.

Happy New Year!

PERSONAL REFLECTIONS

APPLICATION

PERSONAL PRAYER

ADDITIONAL NOTES

RESOLUTION 26
O Give Thanks

SATURATED WORD: Psalm 107:1 - *O give thanks unto the LORD, for he is good: for his mercy endureth forever.*

ISSUE: Jesus is truly the reason for this season. John 3:16 says, "For God so loved the world that he gave his only begotten Son, that whosoever believeth in him should not perish but have everlasting life." Jesus came to redeem us from the penalty of sin. Romans 6:23 says, "For the wages of sin is death; but the gift of God is eternal life through Jesus Christ our Lord."

CHALLENGE: May Jesus Christ, who is the gift and giver of eternal life be the light that shines the brightest in your lives and homes this Christmas Day and beyond. May He bring awe essence to you during your time of worship and arrest you into His presence as you remain yielded and surrendered to Him. I pray that God's covering, protection, and anointing be with you always as miracles and blessings take place in your life. God promised to always be with you and never forsake you. He is a promise- keeper. May He bestow upon you joy, peace, and happiness in the Holy Ghost. Those are the commodities that He loves to give. As the new year rings in, I decree the new year to be your year of more than enough. May any of your dry seasons and desert places become fully saturated and irrigated with the latter rain of God's precious promises.

Merry Christmas and a Happy New Year!

PERSONAL REFLECTIONS

APPLICATION

PERSONAL PRAYER

ADDITIONAL NOTES

RESOLUTION 27
Down But Not Out

SATURATED WORD: II Corinthians 4:8-9 *We are hard pressed on every side, but not crushed; perplexed, but not in despair; persecuted, but not abandoned; struck down, but not destroyed.*

ISSUE: God has seen your struggles, felt your pain, but rallied your perseverance. Through trials and tribulations, you've had to endure (and you did) as a good soldier. You continue to be like a tree that's planted by the rivers of water declaring, "I shall not be moved." People see what you look like on the outside but have no clue what you've dealt with on the inside. If the truth be told, some, if not most of us, are dealing with one thing or another, just in different ways on different levels.

They see your glory but don't know your story.

They see your public presentation but haven't seen your private pain.

They see you dressed up on the outside but not how torn up you've been on the inside.

They see your victory laps but not your pit stops.

They've seen your sunny days but not your gloomy nights.

So what do you do when there's a gap between your experience and your expectation… when you're not experiencing what you expect?

It challenges your faith.

CHALLENGE: How can you keep your peace, maintain your joy, and remain stable in the midst of your greatest challenges? I believe the answer is: KEEP YOUR FAITH IN GOD! He is faithful. Your faith sends a message to your situations and circumstances and tell them that:

Weeping may endure for a night but joy cometh in the morning.

In all the days of my appointed time will I wait until my change come.

I know He didn't bring me this far just to leave me.

Faith says keep fighting when you feel like giving up.

It'll tell you it's only a test, for a greater testimony.

Your coming out will be greater than your going through.

So don't give up, don't give out, and don't give in to adversities because God will deliver you out of them all.

When you're down, tell yourself, "I'm coming back stronger, more determined, more powerful, tenacious, and more durable."

Down but not out!

PERSONAL REFLECTIONS

_____
_____
_____
_____
_____

APPLICATION

_____
_____
_____
_____
_____

PERSONAL PRAYER

_____
_____
_____
_____
_____

ADDITIONAL NOTES

_____
_____
_____
_____

RESOLUTION 28

Use Words Wisely

SATURATED WORD: Proverbs 18:21: *Death and life are in the power of the tongue: and they that love it shall eat the fruit thereof.*

ISSUE: How are you using your words?

- To build up or to tear down?
- To give life or to bring death?
- To add to or to subtract from?
- To encourage or to discourage?

In the courtroom of law your words can acquit or condemn you. What you say cannot only hurt you but someone else as well. Words can make or break you. Sticks and stones may break your bones, but eventually you heal, but something negatively spoken over your life can scar you forever. Have you ever heard "you're going to grow up to be just like your no good dead beat dad"? If that seed ever catches root that child has the propensity of growing up, being a dead beat dad because death and life is in the power of the tongue. Verbal abuse can change the whole dynamics, fabric and outlook on a person's life. You must use your words carefully, wisely and kindly. Hurting people hurt people. It is a spirit that must be cast down and destroyed.

Proverbs 10:19 - When there are many words, transgression is unavoidable, But he who restrains his lips is wise.

Proverbs 13:3 - The one who guards his mouth preserves his life; The one who opens wide his lips comes to ruin.

Ephesians 4:29 - Do not let any unwholesome talk come out of your mouths, but only what is helpful for building others up according to their needs, that it may benefit those who listen.

CHALLENGE: How will you use your words today? To tear down or to build up? To add to or subtract from? To encourage or discourage? To inspire or dissuade? Words are never empty but they sure can leave you feeling that way. Use the choice of your words in a positive way. "Use words wisely".

PERSONAL REFLECTIONS

APPLICATION

PERSONAL PRAYER

ADDITIONAL NOTES

RESOLUTION 29

The Joy Of The Lord Is My Strength

SATURATED WORD: Nehemiah 8:10 - Nehemiah said, *Go and enjoy choice food and sweet drinks, and send some to those who have nothing prepared. This day is holy to our Lord. Do not grieve, for the joy of the LORD is your strength.*

ISSUE: The Joy of the Lord is a strength builder. There are so many challenges in life today that come to chip, chop and chisel at your strength such as divorce, the death of a love one, the loss of a job, issues in the family and lack of finances. In its success many have become weakened leaving various assignments unfinished, gotten off track with life and in some instances gotten totally derailed. But since the joy OF the Lord is your strength you must take full advantage of this resource that is freely available to those who are experiencing the joy IN the Lord. Accepting Christ as your Lord and Savior gives you the joy IN the Lord. When you are connected with Christ you connect with all of His resources and benefits. They are made available to you with a promise and all of His promises are yes and amen. Joy is not dependent upon situations and circumstances because they will come. But joy is an attitude ignited by faith and thanksgiving.

CHALLENGE: 1 Thessalonians 5:16-18 says 16 Rejoice always, 17 pray without ceasing, 18 give thanks in all circumstances; for this is the will of God in Christ Jesus concerning you. Verse 17 is key. One way to pray without ceasing is to practice giving thanks to God all day long by saying "THANK YOU JESUS". As you go throughout each day saying "THANK YOU JESUS " watch the joy of the Lord strengthen you even when you're going through your toughest trial. Verse 18 says give thanks in all circumstances; for this is the will of God in Christ Jesus concerning you.

PERSONAL REFLECTIONS

_____
_____
_____
_____
_____

APPLICATION

_____
_____
_____
_____
_____

PERSONAL PRAYER

_____
_____
_____
_____
_____

ADDITIONAL NOTES

_____
_____
_____
_____

RESOLUTION 30

The Peace Of God in the Midst of Tribulations

SATURATED WORD: John 16:33 *These things I have spoken unto you, that in me ye might have peace. In the world ye shall have tribulation: but be of good cheer; I have overcome the world.*

ISSUE: This peace of God is the treasure of treasures. It was purchased by Jesus Christ on Calvary's cross. You receive this treasure by trusting in Him in the midst of life's storms. With this peace, you can trust God in every area of your life. If you should ever fall, it's peaceful knowing that He's right there with a safety net to catch you with His everlasting arms. This peace transcends understanding, so your faith must be activated for it to be revealed. It's good knowing that God is always right there to help you when you are being faced with daily challenges. Whether you sense God's presence or not, have the peace of knowing that He is with you every moment and step of the way.

CHALLENGE: Your faith will be challenged and tested to see if you will maintain this peace during the next storm you face. Remember, this is a Divine peace. One that can only be given by God.

PERSONAL REFLECTIONS

_____
_____
_____
_____
_____

APPLICATION

_____
_____
_____
_____
_____

PERSONAL PRAYER

_____
_____
_____
_____
_____

ADDITIONAL NOTES

_____
_____
_____
_____
_____

RESOLUTION 31

Facing The Giants

SATURATED WORD: I Samuel 17:46 - *This day will the Lord deliver thee into mine hand...*

ISSUE: What or who is your GIANT? **God** knows what it takes to get each of us prepared to face our GIANTS. He knows how long to hold us in wait until it's time to release us into our purpose. Everything David had to go through for fifteen years was preparing Him for his appointment. While waiting for his appointment, he had a GIANT to face. Nothing is worse than having a testimony without a test…having a position but possessing no power. Facing our GIANTS many times present doubt in our minds. Those doubts keep us from doing what we should. They detain us, refrain us, and hold us back. GIANTS should not intimidate you because the bigger they are, the harder they fall.

David kept his distance from his giant, not because he was afraid, but because he wanted to give him falling room. So in order for us to defeat our GIANTS, we must stay prepared, inspired, motivated and prayed up.

CHALLENGE: Walk each day by faith. Those who trust in God: Think the unthinkable; Reach for the unreachable; Believe the unbelievable; Hope for the imaginable; Live for the incredible; Achieve the improbable! Your GIANTS must fall! Be a GIANT slayer!!

PERSONAL REFLECTIONS

_____
_____
_____
_____
_____

APPLICATION

_____
_____
_____
_____
_____

PERSONAL PRAYER

_____
_____
_____
_____
_____

ADDITIONAL NOTES

_____
_____
_____
_____

RESOLUTION 32

Rejoice In The Lord

SATURATED WORD: Habakkuk 3:19 - *The Lord God is my strength…*

ISSUE: When our situation seems hopeless and helpless and appears that God is silent, we must yet have joy on the inside. Oftentimes, trusting him means looking beyond what we can see to what He sees. Dark times come upon all of us; that's part of life in a fallen world. As believers, we do not have to worry as those without hope. We must trust God in the dark times, take his hand and go where he leads. Who walks in darkness and has no light? Let him trust in the name of the Lord and rely upon his God. The Lord God is my strength.

CHALLENGE: The next time you find yourself weak, will you rely upon God to be your strength? 2 Corinthians 12:9 *But He said to me, "My grace is sufficient for you, for power is perfected in weakness."* Therefore, I will most gladly boast all the more about my weaknesses, so that Christ's power may reside in me.

PERSONAL REFLECTIONS

_____
_____
_____
_____
_____

APPLICATION

_____
_____
_____
_____
_____

PERSONAL PRAYER

_____
_____
_____
_____
_____

ADDITIONAL NOTES

_____
_____
_____
_____

RESOLUTION 33

A Continuous Prayer Life

SATURATED WORD: Luke 18:1 - *And he spake a parable unto them to this end, that men ought always to pray, and not to faint.*

ISSUE: Prayer is communion and conversation with God. One thing we eventually learn about relationships is that they must increase or they will decrease. Only a rare relationship can remain the same. One of the things that causes the relationships to grow is honesty in communication. As it relates to prayer, God wants closeness, commitment and companionship with us. Since prayer is our main means of communicating with God, it is imperative that we increase the effectiveness of our prayer life. Prayer time will always increase when we give God equal time to speak. Prayer time is not a start and stop but must become a continuous part of our lifestyle since it is our lifeline. Never put prayer off for tomorrow for what needs to be done today because we need God every day. Have a set time and a set place each and every day where you and God meet.

CHALLENGE: Never stand God up and have Him waiting at your prayer time and place and you never show up. A continuous prayer life is essential in enabling you not to faint.

PERSONAL REFLECTIONS

APPLICATION

PERSONAL PRAYER

ADDITIONAL NOTES

RESOLUTION 34

Keep Your Prayer Wheel Turning

SATURATED WORD: 1 Thessalonian 5:17 - *Pray without ceasing.*

ISSUE: Any Christian who is seeking council for the success in fulfilling the great commission is given these words, "much prayer, much power, little prayer, little power." Regardless of what part we play in advancing the kingdom of God, a primary prerequisite to an effective outcome is an effective prayer life. Not understanding the principles that govern prayer has caused many Christians to be ineffective in their prayer life. Such prayerlessness stifles our ability to receive the continuous flow of Divine power necessary to be effective in God's service. Prayerlessness causes us to become fruitless Christians.

CHALLENGE: If you fail fruit inspection, check out your prayer life to see if your prayer wheel is still turning

PERSONAL REFLECTIONS

_____
_____
_____
_____
_____

APPLICATION

_____
_____
_____
_____
_____

PERSONAL PRAYER

_____
_____
_____
_____
_____

ADDITIONAL NOTES

_____
_____
_____
_____

RESOLUTION 35
Take It To The Lord In Prayer

SATURATED WORD: Romans 12:12 - *Be joyful in hope, patient in affliction, faithful in prayer*.

ISSUE: When problems begin taking over your thoughts causing you to grow weary and feeling defeated, you need someone whom you can turn to that has the ability to turn things around and bring about positive results. Jesus is your answer. You will always face trouble in this life but more importantly is to know that you don't have to face it alone. The more challenging things become, the more you can depend upon Him to solve them. Life is a series of problem-solving opportunities. The problems you face will either defeat you or develop you - depending on how you respond to them. God uses problems to DIRECT you - INSPECT you - CORRECT you - PROTECT you - and PERFECT you. Problems, when responded to correctly, are character builders. Although uncomfortable, God is far more interested in your character than your comfort. Your relationship to God and your character are the only two things you're going to take with you into eternity.

CHALLENGE: Problems help us learn to be patient. Patience develops strength of character in us and helps us trust God more each time we use it.

PERSONAL REFLECTIONS

_____
_____
_____
_____
_____

APPLICATION

_____
_____
_____
_____
_____

PERSONAL PRAYER

_____
_____
_____
_____
_____

ADDITIONAL NOTES

_____
_____
_____
_____

RESOLUTION 36
Expect An Expected End

SATURATED WORD: Jeremiah 29:11 - *For I know the thoughts that I think toward you, saith the Lord, thoughts of peace, and not of evil, to give you an expected end.*

ISSUE: What do you expect in the end? Since you cannot see your future, you must trust God - the one who holds it. Depend upon his wisdom to guide you through these unchartered waters. God has your future all planned out. Open your ears to His voice and your eyes to his vision. Focus on where he wants you to go. He will give you the courage to steer your life in His direction, but you must stay the course. As He gives directions, you must move forward even while sailing in unknown waters. He has commanded us to advance. When we sail toward him, we take possession of the blessings He has already provided for us.

* Do you have high expectations for your future?

* What is your expected end?

* Which direction are you moving in life? Forward or backwards?

* If you could change one thing in your life, what would it be? (Your future could depend upon it).

CHALLENGE: As you continue to follow God's lead, know that you will end up in the perfect place of your purpose and destiny.

PERSONAL REFLECTIONS

_____
_____
_____
_____
_____

APPLICATION

_____
_____
_____
_____
_____

PERSONAL PRAYER

_____
_____
_____
_____
_____

ADDITIONAL NOTES

_____
_____
_____
_____

RESOLUTION 37
Forward Looking Faith

SATURATED WORD: Mark 11:24 - *Therefore I say unto you, what things so ever ye desire, when ye pray, believe that ye receive them, and ye shall have them.*

ISSUE: Faith is the substance of things hoped for, the evidence of things not seen.

* What is your faith looking forward to?

* Do you have the faith that what you're believing God for shall surely come to pass?

* Are you sure that what you're believing God for is in His will and purpose for your life?

This is a time for you to position and anchor yourself firmly and faithfully on the word of God. Remove anything that can hinder or stifle your expectation for greater in your life. Your dependency must be upon God in every way.

Without faith it's impossible to please Him. What things so ever you desire, when you pray, believe that you receive them and you shall have them. When you give those things to God, you must believe that those things which you say shall come to pass and you shall have whatsoever you said.

CHALLENGE: Too often you try to do things in your own strength and might, but learn to trust in the Lord with all of your heart and lean not unto your own understanding, and in all your ways acknowledge Him, and He will direct your path.

* MAY YOUR FAITH FAIL NOT!!
* KEEP FAITHFULLY LOOKING FORWARD!!
* TRUST GOD ONE DAY AT A TIME!!

PERSONAL REFLECTIONS

_____
_____
_____
_____
_____

APPLICATION

_____
_____
_____
_____
_____

PERSONAL PRAYER

_____
_____
_____
_____
_____

ADDITIONAL NOTES

_____
_____
_____
_____

RESOLUTION 38

More Than Conquerors

SATURATED WORD: Romans 8:37 - *Nay, in all these things we are more than conquerors through him that loved us.*

ISSUE: Are you a conqueror or are you being conquered? Are you a victim or a victor? We might as well face it, we're in a war. But the war we're in is already won. Therefore, we must continue to fight the good fight of faith. Remember, the battle is not yours, but the Lord's. As believers, the enemy attacks us and tries to defeat us with afflictions, distress, persecution, famine, tribulations, and many other things, but we are not only conquerors but more than conquerors -- not only over sin and satan but over all of the reproaches of this world. The power of Christ that is in you shall do what the presence of Christ did when he walked the earth. We walk in His power and authority, not as defeated foes, but mighty conquerors made possible by the redemptive work on Calvary's cross. We lost a garden produced by sin, but we gained a heaven made possible by Jesus' death, burial, and resurrection.

CHALLENGE: Keep fighting the good fight of faith. Come what may, "nay in all these things we are more than conquerors through Him that loved us.

PERSONAL REFLECTIONS

_____
_____
_____
_____
_____

APPLICATION

_____
_____
_____
_____
_____

PERSONAL PRAYER

_____
_____
_____
_____
_____

ADDITIONAL NOTES

_____
_____
_____
_____

RESOLUTION 39

Get Back Up Again

SATURATED WORD: Proverb 24:16 - *For a righteous man falleth seven times, and riseth up again; But the wicked are overthrown by calamity.*

ISSUE: It's important to remember that setbacks, failures, and tragedies are all part of life. Whether we manage to find joy and success in the daily struggles is largely dependent upon our ability to persevere through even the toughest adversities without ever giving up. Fall seven times, stand up eight! Important, because it can make the present moment less difficult to bear. If we believe that tomorrow will be better, we can bear our hardships today. Our hardships today prepare us for what's coming ahead.

CHALLENGE: Everybody experiences down days, but don't allow them to become your fate. Don't stay down, but get back up again!

PERSONAL REFLECTIONS

_____
_____
_____
_____
_____

APPLICATION

_____
_____
_____
_____
_____

PERSONAL PRAYER

_____
_____
_____
_____
_____

ADDITIONAL NOTES

_____
_____
_____
_____

RESOLUTION 40

Stay Calm In The Storm

SATURATED WORD: Mark 4:39 - *And he arose, and rebuked the wind, and said unto the sea, Peace, be still. And the wind ceased, and there was a great calm.*

ISSUE: Storms are inevitable, but they're no stranger to Jesus. He walked them, sailed them, and spoke to them, saying "PEACE BE STILL." The wind obeyed his authority and power causing a great calm to take place. DO YOU NEED A GREAT CALM IN YOUR STORM TODAY? The same Jesus that spoke peace to the wind and the sea will speak peace to the wind of the sea of your mind, marriage, job, children, health, finance, or relationship and help you to avoid the shipwreck you're heading for. HOW WILL YOU REACT TO YOUR NEXT STORM? Will you panic and jump ship, be paralyzed by fear, or trust Jesus?

CHALLENGE: Stay calm right in the eye of the storm if you can trust Jesus enough to speak to it. You won't always be taken out of the storm. REMEMBER: For we walk by faith and not by sight.

PERSONAL REFLECTIONS

_____
_____
_____
_____
_____

APPLICATION

_____
_____
_____
_____
_____

PERSONAL PRAYER

_____
_____
_____
_____
_____

ADDITIONAL NOTES

_____
_____
_____
_____

RESOLUTION 41

Go For It Now

SATURATED WORD: Proverbs 6:4 - *Don't put it off; do it now! Don't rest until you do.*

ISSUE: There are things in life that will tackle you, but you can't afford to stay down. You must get back up, dust yourself off, and get ready for the next play. You were born to win, but many have been conditioned to lose. You've got to recognize that you have tremendous potential inside of you, full of life's purpose. But you've got to uncover it in order to discover it.

Two-thirds of God's name is go. So stop putting off for tomorrow for what you can do today. Get ready, set. and go for it! Today is now, tomorrow is then, and yesterday is when. You can't go back to when. Tomorrow is then. All you have is now.

CHALLENGE: What are you waiting for? Go on and get started on your dreams, goals and visions. You have great potential.! Go for it NOW! Destiny is waiting!

PERSONAL REFLECTIONS

APPLICATION

PERSONAL PRAYER

ADDITIONAL NOTES

RESOLUTION 42

All Things Are Working For Your Good

SATURATED WORD: Romans 8:28 - *And we know that all things work together for good to them that love God, to them who are the called according to his purpose.*

ISSUE: Because God said ALL THINGS work together for good, that includes what you are dealing with or going through right now as well. It doesn't have to be good in order for God to take it and make it work together for good. If its some things you brought upon yourself, then repent, be restored, and go in another direction. Make a right turn and go straight. If you keep doing what you've been doing, you'll keep getting what you've been getting, so change directions.

> * The Apostle Paul said that the power of God works best in weakness. So he boasted about his weaknesses because through it, the power of Christ could work through him.
>
> * Be thankful for your struggles because without them you would not have stumbled across God's strength.

CHALLENGE: Ask God for forgiveness in every area of your life and allow Him to restore all the years you've lost through worry, unforgiveness, malice, hate, fear, etc. Remember, whatever God allows you to GET TO, he will allow you to GET THROUGH. It doesn't matter how bad things get, God can cause them to work together for good to them that love God, to them who are called according to His purpose.

PERSONAL REFLECTIONS

_____
_____
_____
_____
_____

APPLICATION

_____
_____
_____
_____
_____

PERSONAL PRAYER

_____
_____
_____
_____
_____

ADDITIONAL NOTES

_____
_____
_____
_____

RESOLUTION 43

Live Life Purposefully

SATURATED WORD: James 4:14 - *Whereas ye know not what shall be on the morrow. For what is your life? It is even a vapour, that appeareth for a little time, and then vanisheth away."*

ISSUE: Life is the period of time between birth and death. Life can be here today and gone tomorrow. A lot of people have life but are not living. When you are not living, you're only existing. You become just a fixture in the earth when you should be a mover and shaker. When you're really living, you're walking in purpose. And when you're walking in your purpose, your purpose will lead you to your destiny. And at your destiny, was life better because you were here?

CHALLENGE: Live life purposefully, positionally, prayerfully and prosperously. Enough time has passed. Live life now, on purpose

PERSONAL REFLECTIONS

_____
_____
_____
_____
_____

APPLICATION

_____
_____
_____
_____
_____

PERSONAL PRAYER

_____
_____
_____
_____

ADDITIONAL NOTES

_____
_____
_____
_____

RESOLUTION 44

Win Souls For God's Kingdom

SATURATED WORD: Luke 14:23 - *And the Lord said unto the servant, "Go out into the highways and hedges, and compel them to come in, that my house may be filled."*

ISSUE: We as the body of Christ are an extension of Jesus in the earth realm. Jesus was here on a temporary assignment to unite man to God and God to man. We as the body of Christ are to continue where he left off. Sinners don't need a turn away; they need a turnaround. Every sinner is a saved one's assignment. Look at your hands. Do you see any blood on them?

CHALLENGE: Ask God to make you a soul-winning magnet for the kingdom of God.

PERSONAL REFLECTIONS

APPLICATION

PERSONAL PRAYER

ADDITIONAL NOTES

RESOLUTION 45

One Step At A Time

SATURATED WORD: Proverbs 3:5-6 - *Trust in the Lord with all thine heart; and lean not unto thine own understanding. In all thy ways acknowledge him, and he shall direct thy paths.*

ISSUE: Let God lead and guide you step by step as you walk purposefully with Him throughout each day. Trust him enough to face problems as they come, rather than trying to anticipate them. He will guide you safely through each day, but you can find Him only in the present. All that God requires of us is to follow him one step at a time. The steps of a good man are ordered by the Lord.

CHALLENGE: Allow the Lord to order your steps, one step at a time.

PERSONAL REFLECTIONS

_____
_____
_____
_____
_____

APPLICATION

_____
_____
_____
_____
_____

PERSONAL PRAYER

_____
_____
_____
_____
_____

ADDITIONAL NOTES

_____
_____
_____
_____

RESOLUTION 46

The Best Knocker

SATURATED WORD: Matthew 7:7 - *Ask and it shall be given you; seek, and he shall find; knock, and it shall be opened.*

ISSUE: The strongest in God's kingdom is he who is the best knocker. If you knock, He will answer. When the door is opened and He's standing on the other side, what then? Whenever we make a request of Him, we expect a response. Likewise, whenever He knocks at your door, He expects a response. When he knocks, do you answer? Well, He's knocking now! Will you open up and let Him in or will He be left standing outside? Are you willing to give a response to His request?

CHALLENGE: Questions to ponder:

- Am I a good knocker?
- Am I a good host whenever He comes to visit?
- Do I make Him feel welcomed?
- Is He coming into a clean house or do I need to clear some things up?

PERSONAL REFLECTIONS

APPLICATION

PERSONAL PRAYER

ADDITIONAL NOTES

RESOLUTION 47

Be Content

SATURATED WORD: Philippians 4.11 - *Not that I speak from want, for I have learned to be content in whatever circumstances I am.*

ISSUE: The Apostle Paul said, "I've learned to be content in whatever state I'm in." If the things you're doing don't make you happy, then you're not happy. But you can be content, even when the things that make you happy are not happening. Happiness is feeling good about what you're doing or about what you have, but contentment is being happy with who you are. Happiness is about the "what," and contentment is about the "who." Happiness is about when others are treating you well or when circumstances are going in your favor, but contentment comes from knowing that God is in control regardless of your circumstances or situations. People who are never satisfied with themselves are never satisfied with others. The steps of a good man are ordered by the Lord. Steps are for inclining or declining. When you make a step in God, it is not merely a single step, but it is a turnaround. In God it means that you're coming to a higher level. Contentment doesn't mean that you won't have problems, but it means that problems won't have you. Happiness is temporary, but contentment is lasting. Whatever you give your attention to, you will create more of. If you think on the deliverance of God in the past, you'll get more if it in the future. Sometimes we're so busy adding up our troubles until we forget to count our blessings.

CHALLENGE: Whatever you may be going through, find your contentment in God.

PERSONAL REFLECTIONS

___

APPLICATION

___

PERSONAL PRAYER

___

ADDITIONAL NOTES

___

RESOLUTION 48

Conquer What's Conquering You

SATURATED WORD: Psalm 51:10 - *Create in me a clean heart, O God; and renew a right spirit within me.*

ISSUE: King David was a great military conqueror, but he could not conquer himself. He realized that the only good in him was the God in him. When we think of the life of King David, several things come to mind. We know him as a fearless shepherd, a giant slayer, a warrior, a king, a man after God's own heart, and one who was included in the Faith Hall of Fame. With all of his strengths, he also had weaknesses. One of the biggest highlights of his weaknesses was when he committed adultery with Bathsheba. He tried to cover up her pregnancy and when he failed, he had her husband Uriah killed. Not only was his sin highlighted, but his repentance as well.

We find in Psalm 51: He asked God for mercy, to wash him thoroughly from his iniquity, and to cleanse him from his sin. He acknowledged his transgressions. He asked God, "Purge me with hyssop, and I shall be clean: wash me, and I shall be whiter than snow. Create in me a clean heart, O God; and renew a right spirit within me. Restore unto me the joy of my salvation." His repentance was not just, " I'm sorry; I'll try to do better the next time" sort of thing, but a deep, heartfelt plea to God for forgiveness, healing and restoration.

CHALLENGE: You will never find strength or be able to conquer what's conquering you without repentance and restoration. So repent and be restored. That's how you conquer what's conquering you!

PERSONAL REFLECTIONS

_____
_____
_____
_____
_____

APPLICATION

_____
_____
_____
_____
_____

PERSONAL PRAYER

_____
_____
_____
_____
_____

ADDITIONAL NOTES

_____
_____
_____
_____

RESOLUTION 49

Don't Journey Without God

SATURATED WORD: Proverb 3:5-6 - *Trust in the Lord with all your heart and lean not unto your own understanding, but in all your ways acknowledge Him and he shall direct your path.*

ISSUE: As you travel through life, you might not know what's on the road ahead, but God will equip you for the journey. Even when you can't trace Him, you've got to trust Him! Watch the road signs along the way because one wrong turn can cause you to be lost.

CHALLENGE: Don't travel through life without God. Take Him with you everywhere you go.

PERSONAL REFLECTIONS

_____
_____
_____
_____
_____

APPLICATION

_____
_____
_____
_____
_____

PERSONAL PRAYER

_____
_____
_____
_____
_____

ADDITIONAL NOTES

_____
_____
_____
_____

RESOLUTION 50

My Daily Declaration

SATURATED WORD: John 14:27 - *Peace I leave with you, My peace I give to you; not as the world gives do I give to you. Let not your heart be troubled, neither let it be afraid.*

ISSUE: My mind is clothed and covered with the mind of Christ, and I wear his thoughts throughout each day. I have the peace of God which passeth all understanding. The Holy Spirit controls my thinking through the transformation of my renewed mind. I let go all cares and worries and replace them with God's presence and peace. Trusting and relying upon God are the keys to my peace and provisions. In Him I live, move, and have my being.

CHALLENGE: Make daily declarations to daily empower your life.

PERSONAL REFLECTIONS

APPLICATION

PERSONAL PRAYER

ADDITIONAL NOTES

RESOLUTION 51

New Life In Christ

SATURATED WORD: Ephesians 4:24 - *And that he put on the new man, which after God is created in righteousness and true holiness.*

ISSUE: New life is a very familiar term, especially to Christians. There are churches and ministries in various denominations with the name New Life. But this new life is more than a church name or denomination. It is a life, going from being conformed to this world to being transformed by the renewing of your mind that you may prove what is good, and acceptable, and perfect will of God. With this new life comes responsibilities and accountability. We are accountable to the Giver of this gift which is in Christ Jesus. Our responsibility must be to live this New Life according to His word. Some people believe that this new life is available only for now. Others believe that it is reserved for us in the future, but this new life in Christ is available to whosoever will, right now. What you must know is that this new life requires some adjustments, alignments, and learning. There has to be some adjustments to your will, mind, and emotion. You are moving from being conformed to this world to being transformed by the renewing of your mind and emotion. With this new life in Christ, your life must be in alignment with the word of God. You must learn by studying His word. One thing we must do after acquiring this new life is to put off the old man. We must get free of all bad habits and sinful attitudes when we take on this brand new life. The former life is a corrupt life based on sinful desires and thoughts that come from a mind that is empty and alienated from God. The life of the old man is a life with no true joy or peace of mind. Trying to endure this new life with old habits is what keeps many people from fully enjoying the abundant life that is now available to them in Christ. So we must set our affections and thoughts on things above, forgetting those things which are behind, and live according to God's will and purpose for our lives.

CHALLENGE: Do you want to have this new life in Christ? Do you want to be connected to the source that gives eternal life? Are you convinced today that it's time to get rid of the old man and put on the new? Have you been straddling the fence? Find this new life in Christ that the Father so liberally gives.

PERSONAL REFLECTIONS

_____
_____
_____
_____
_____

APPLICATION

_____
_____
_____
_____
_____

PERSONAL PRAYER

_____
_____
_____
_____
_____

ADDITIONAL NOTES

_____
_____
_____
_____

RESOLUTION 52

Trust The Process

SATURATED WORD: Proverbs 14:12 - *There is a way which seemeth right unto a man, but the end thereof are the ways of death*

ISSUE: I was driving in a city where the routes were very unfamiliar to me. I was using a GPS which had been pretty dependable and served me well over the years. I came to a certain point in my travel and the woman on the GPS said to make a right turn. Making a right turn seemed misleading and that it would take me in the wrong direction. Wanting to be sure, I pulled over into a gas station to seek directions from the attendant there. To my amazement, he gave me the same instructions that the GPS had given me. So I decided to yield myself to the instructions even though I felt that it was taking me the wrong way. As I was driving along that route, the GPS began taking me down some small winding roads into a couple of small communities that gave the appearance that I was lost. I thought that at that point I should have been on a much larger highway with multiple lanes, but instead, I was driving on a very narrow single lane with no room to spare. As time went on, this road that appeared to be misleading, suddenly merged onto the freeway that I was trying to get on from the start. I ended up further ahead than if I had gone the way that I thought. What happened was I didn't trust the process of the leading of the GPS. There were many things that looked so unfamiliar to me that I thought I was going wrong, but In fact, the GPS was really leading me the right way. The Bible has been said by many to be "Basic Instructions Before Leaving Earth." It is defined as the inspired, infallible Word of God. It is the roadmap from earth to eternity. There are times when God is speaking to us from His Word when we think things should be done another way. He clearly tells us in Isaiah 55:8, "For my thoughts are not your thoughts, neither are your ways my ways, saith the Lord." Proverbs 14:12 says, "There is a way which seemeth right unto a man, but the end thereof are the ways of death." God is never misleading, even when we don't understand the process. The children of Israel marched around the walls of Jericho once for six days and on the seventh day they marched seven times. They gave a great shout, the trumpeters blasted their horns, and the walls of Jericho began to fall flat as they took over the city. They took God's Word and followed the process. Maybe there were some who felt like God should have made them a stronger army or strengthened their armor, but instead, He chose another way that gave them the victory.

CHALLENGE: Whatever God is saying to you today, whatever directions He is giving you to follow, trust the process and you will end up where you should be, and that is in the perfect will of God. Let today be your day to go all the way with the Lord by accepting this new life in Christ Jesus.

PERSONAL REFLECTIONS

_____
_____
_____
_____
_____

APPLICATION

_____
_____
_____
_____
_____

PERSONAL PRAYER

_____
_____
_____
_____
_____

ADDITIONAL NOTES

_____
_____
_____
_____

MEET THE AUTHOR

Ronald B. Engram is a native of Macon, Georgia and upon graduating from high school, he also lived in Atlanta, Georgia and Detroit, Michigan. He is the husband of First Lady Emy Carlita Bautista Engram. He is the son of the late Deacon James Engram and Mother Amy L. Engram, State Supervisor of Southern GA Second Ecclesiastical Jurisdiction. He is the brother of Evangelist Missionary Cynthia Cooper, and Pastor Dr. Brenda Engram Salter. Bishop-Designee Engram was called into the ministry and did his first sermon in November 1999. In 2002 he was ordained as an Elder in the Southern GA Second Ecclesiastical Jurisdiction under the leadership of Bishop Jack Stephens. He has been fortunate as a Minister and Elder to serve under the leadership of former Pastors of Ash Street such as the late Bishop Cephas Hicks, Elder William Green, and Elder Marshall Randolph where Bishop-Designee Engram served as his Assistant Pastor. In November 2007, Bishop-Designee Engram became interim Pastor and in March 2008 he was installed officially pastor of Ash Street COGIC. On the Jurisdictional level, Pastor Engram served formerly as secretary of the Pastors and Elders Council and the Board of Ordination for Southern GA Second Ecclesiastical Jurisdiction. On the district level, Pastor Engram served under the leadership of Regional Superintendent Lewis Releford Jr. as the chairman and former secretary of the Macon District Churches of God in Christ. Bishop-Designee Engram's elevation to Superintendent was appointed by Bishop J. Wayne Leggett of Southern Georgia Second Ecclesiastical Jurisdiction in 2018. He was appointed Bishop-Designee of Southern GA Second Ecclesiastical Jurisdiction in June 2020. He is the founder of the Young Men Ambassadors for Christ, and implemented from the national to the local church the "Young Men of Valor." He completed courses in Business Administration from Atlanta Area Tech, a graduate of Armstrong's Supervisors Of The Future in Lancaster Pennsylvania, Completed Leadership courses from Penn State University, studied spiritual counseling from the America Association of Christian Counseling, and is a graduate of C.H. Mason Seminary. He has been a passionate writer since he was a child. At the age of 10, he knew that someday he would author books.

Bishop-Designee Engram is committed to motivating the increasing of faith among the believers. He propels people to fulfill their destiny with purpose, while walking in righteousness, holiness, and integrity.

www.ingramcontent.com/pod-product-compliance
Lightning Source LLC
LaVergne TN
LVHW021352080426
835508LV00020B/2248